contents

forward

When I was in the seventh grade, I was sitting at the lunch table with a bunch of girls. Someone next to me nudged my arm and passed me a wad of folded paper, torn from a notebook. "Have you seen this yet?" She asked. I opened it up and had an immediate visceral reaction when I saw the first lines of a sophomoric crush poem that I had recently penned and shared with a friend. It was copied over in another's hand and there was no signature of authorship. I guess that was the moment I became a published poet.

In college, I sat through interminable writing workshops, studying how to use metaphor and simile, how to rewrite and break up lines, how to critique, etc. After college, I put my poetry back into a secret place and began to teach school and sing the songs of others in bars and coffee shops. I continued to write, thinking of my poems as watercolors. Eventually, I started to write and perform my own songs, allowing that to more or less pay my rent and make my way in the world. I fell madly in love with the troubadour's life and the myriad of other poets and bohemians I meet along the way.

For these past twenty years, I have been privileged to perform for many wonderful audiences all over the United States and Canada as well as to teach writing and performing to college students. Several years ago, one of my fans challenged me to publish a poem on my monthly newsletter and the response was so great that I created a tradition.

So…here's my first ever collection of poems, gleaned from a big pile of journals, and lovingly edited by Rachel Barenblat, fellow poet and founder of Inkberry.org in North Adams, MA. As I look through this collection,

I'm amazed by all the places these poems came through... Boulder, Omega Institute, Kripalu Center, Arizona, New Zealand, Africa, Asheville, Maine, the Cincinnati Airport, and of course, right here at home in the Berkshires.

I'd like to thank Bruce Gershkowitz, the subject of that first sophomoric poem, wherever he may be, I'd like to thank Max and Susie Ochs, for making a deal with me, and Elissa Klein, for turning these pages into a book.

How to Make Mud Pie Soup

First
go to the coffee shop
and get a large latte to go

Then drive to the playground
park
and get down on all fours
sift through the pebbles and rocks with your hands
putting leaves and other debris to the side
for flavoring
make sure your knees get very very dirty

While the soup is cooking
run across the monkey bridge twice
go down the big slide
don't be afraid
hold hands and sing

The soup is always ready
just before nap time
don't worry
there's plenty for everyone

A Different Animal

Oded was Israeli
a jazz musician
who painted his walls in yellow and orange polka dots
to make up for a loveless childhood

We would sit together under the eaves
guitars on our laps
and talk about other people we knew

Whenever we reached the conclusion
that no one can truly be understood
he would look right at me
tap his forehead with his index finger
and say "my friend, a different animal"

You and I
rail against truths
trying so hard to change each other
instead of looking at ourselves

Over the years
we have become experts
on each other's faults

stray beard hairs in the sink
unaccountable mood swings
consistent lateness
each of these ammunition
in a war as old as the middle east

perhaps it would be better to combine forces
find an eave to sit under
and tap our own foreheads gently

saying, with grace
and the smallest possible iota of understanding
"my friend, a different animal."

Primary Maternal Pre-Occupation

So here I am
amidst aisles and aisles of choices
as if I knew what distinguished
a Huggies from a Pampers

Women walk by
their carts are always full
several of them have two carts
they are pushing one and pulling the other
all of them have babies
...except for the pregnant ones

No one even glances at me
Clearly they think I am one of them
they cannot seem to tell
that I am a foreigner in this land

On the list from the adoption agency
I have been instructed to bring
formula
clothing
a hat
a stroller
diapers
wipes
bottles
cups
a blankie
and three one pound cans of Folger's coffee
for the officials

everyone has been a parent
I have fielded so much advice
and I could spend forever in this Wal-Mart
searching desperately for a rubber sheet
or a pair of little mittens

So here I am
world traveler
backpacker
brown rice and veggie eater
just a glass of red wine and a salad gal
trying to decide between the transparent teether
and the solid blue gel ring
wondering about the size of her feet and her bottom

outside
the same sun is shining
a new crop of leaves drift toward the ground
wind whistles and sighs
laughing at me
seeker
poet
wanderer
soon to be set down solidly
on the path of true adventure
motherhood
and take my place
amidst these other Wal-Mart shoppers

Mariah Colorado

We named you after a river
your father and I
because we waited a long time to find you
because we knew you would run through the center of our lives
carrying the things all humans need to survive
sand and silt
driftwood
wildlife
reflection
white waves
foam
heavy boulders
the tiny pebbles that creep along the bottom
love
and even the mad bubbling spaces
you cannot touch or grab
but must merely hold your breath
and swim through

Ba

indisputably the only word
our one year old daughter knows for sure

in the morning
she will cuddle for a few short moments
and then fix you with her wide-eyed stare and says "ba?"
only you know it's not a question

you fumble for your bottoms
hop out of bed into the kitchen
trying to pour and heat
before the whining escalates
oh
the relief when you put it in her tiny little hands
"oh ba" she says
"ah ba"

the world of ba turns out to be quite wide
jars of spaghetti sauce
and gallon jugs of spring water
are also ba
she sees them lined up on shelves at the supermarket
and she imagines herself to be in ba heaven
at home, she tears through the recycling bin when I am not looking
she tips the empty apple juice container to her mouth

the bathtub is ba turned inside out
she rolls in it, oogles and jabbers
she crawls to both ends looking for the cup I use to rinse her hair
she fills it with bath water
and swallows as much as possible
before I take it away

it's a simple life...
all that is ba
and all that is not ba

after all
what is a language for?

Paper

Everywhere I look I am surrounded by paper
and it's not just me
It's everywhere

Kitchen tables
credenzas
next to the commode

not love letters
or pictures of beautiful places
but red ink warnings
that I have slipped again
miles expiring
taxes overdue
big sale ending Saturday
rsvp asap
how to program your new state of the art remote control
date books
printouts
passports
postage
all so very important

If I didn't have so much paper to attend to
I'd have time to go walking amongst the trees

I used to be a poet
but now I am
efficient

A Googolplex

On the way to Thanksgiving dinner

Eight year old Forrest tries to get his little cousin to count

"Can you count to one hundred?" he asks

"I can count to a googolplex," she answers

We all snicker

"Did you know that if you started counting the day you
were born and lived to be one hundred years old, and
you never stopped counting, you still couldn't count a
googolplex?"

Silence

"and did you know" he continues, "that in the whole
world, there isn't a googolplex of anything...not grains of
sand or stars or anything?"

Silence again

"What about love?" his little cousin asks

We all hold our breaths

The truth always stuns us into silence

Pennsylvania

Right now the only problem I have
is entirely too much Pennsylvania

From the border at Youngstown
to the perky point at Port Jervis
the interstate lumbers along
new speed limits creating an obnoxious impatience

I set the cruise at seventy
and let the eager speeders sit on my bumper
while I pass the truck, the tree, grandma

I push my scan button
and a Christian man takes credit
for teaching a street kid how to pray
I push it again
and it circles like a slot machine
only to land in the same place-
Pennsylvania

At the rest area
a man of color opens his car door
and throws a hot cup of coffee out onto the pavement
we have matching Hondas

Just a moment later
the maintenance man comes by
to empty the garbage

He picks up the empty cup
cusses the man of color
He tells me that they don't deserve to live in this country

I agree with him about the man's behavior
but I cannot fault his color
his immigration status
or even his taste in cars
and maybe we suffer the same affliction -
strangers
alone in the dawn
with entirely too much Pennsylvania

All the Dolls

Somewhere along the way
Baby Ling lost her pants
They were velour and fuchsia
I wanted a pair of pants like that

She says she is going to tell Madeleine about China, and
the Grand Canyon
In exchange, Madeleine will show Baby Ling her scar
and teach her how to speak French
because she's from France
and everyone knows that that's the best place

Ariel will show us all how to swim
and comb your hair with a fork
Groovy girl has her own sleeping bag
and Barbie...
well, no one knows what Barbie will tell us
underneath her sequined silver swim suit
she seems to retain the formula for perpetual youth
no cellulite
no stretch marks

all the dolls
have secrets to share

Flower Girl

She is so excited
She tells everyone at school
even though she has no idea what it means

The groom watches the Weather Channel all night
the day of the wedding dawns wet and grey
a hurricane blows its way up the coast
and we are catching its tail end

globs of rain big enough to fill teaspoons
fall on the manicured lawns
and send us scurrying back to our closets for wool and goretex
but she pulls down taffeta, lilac, pink

all the dresses she's trying to decide between
while we sit there in our polypropylene

at 4:01 PM we see a hole in the sky
seats are dried off and replaced
the bride kisses her carefully dyed to match shoes goodbye
and my daughter begins her first march down the aisle

She takes this assignment seriously
with her utmost attention
she follows the fiddler
strewing daisy petals before her

right, then left
then right again
barely looking up to see the afternoon sun
beginning its anticipated emergence

Only she and the bride stay the course
enduring sleevelessness
brocaded and tiaraed
sporting goosebumps alongside taffeta and lace

One cannot compromise fashion
for such mundanely mortal sufferings
as wet
and cold

The sky clears with the vows
We ooh and ah as rings are exchanged
The newlyweds will always tell this story

The flower girl runs across the lawn, climbing over rocks
to join the other children
ready now to mix mud with brocade, lace, love
and more rain

Doors

I went to see you in your new old house
a converted garage from a time when woodwork
was more than a trip to Home Depot
gorgeous paneling ensconced your cranky heater
and your dysfunctional kitchen

I slept on a mattress on the hard wood floor
in a room so small that the door was at my ear

hung years ago
it could not be opened without scraping against the floor
leaving a mark
both visible and audible

if I closed it tightly
it would open each time you closed yours
and if I left it cracked open
you would close your door tightly

our doors
seem to have a relationship

Funeral for a Bakery

Of course
all the jazz musicians are there
sans instruments
sporting awkward hands
either stuffed in pockets
or gesticulating sadly

The chalkboard facing the street simply says "ciao"
but customers keep coming through the door
ringing the little bell
unaware of the elegant death about to transpire
they ask about bread
shake their middle class heads
and leave with cake

Heather, the proprietor who could not make rent
in our trendy little town
smiles and passes out free coffee

Soon there will be another art gallery
I like art
but how will I use it to make a smoked turkey sandwich
for my daughter to take to pre-school?
Wouldn't the addition of mayo and mustard
Somehow seem redundant?

I lean across the glass cases to wish Heather well
I'm feeling emotional
I've always been grateful to those willing to rise early enough
to see that the rest of us eat
I would've given her a break in rent
but I'm not a landlord
just another musician
gesticulating sadly

A Rainy Day

My maternal grandmother was a seamstress.
"Times were hard then," they tell me.
"She used to remove stitches carefully from each hem and seam,
so she could reuse the thread."

"I am the dream she had," I tell myself,
staring off across these padded hills
donning my leather jacket
and climbing into my perfect Japanese car.

"I am the place she could never imagine going," I claim,
driving into a town that greets me, cheers me on,
delivers my junk mail on time.

No one shows up at my door to demand their share
No late-night interrogation, no pogrom
No one requisitions the bicycle hanging in my garage
or the oranges in the beautiful bowl on my counter.

But the crimes of the past still course through me
I try to use up each small bit of food in my cupboard
I clip the coupons that bring me bargains
I pick up fallen pennies because I tell myself that I need the luck

I fight the good fight and wonder
I hide myself behind this gate of plenty
hoarding blessings for a rainy day.

Waiting for Penguins

Even though the guide book says that they were once pests
we fork over our colored money
and take our seats on the newly constructed bleachers
under an aluminum roof

women in green uniforms herd us up and away
and explain the rules of viewing
there are fences to mind
flash cameras to be tamed
noise kept to a minimum

when they finish speaking, there is quiet
the moon has risen full over the ocean
waves break on rocks
the women in green scan the horizon
and whisper into walkie-talkies

they do this every night

finally there is a squeak and a squawk
the young, fat birds emerge from their hillside nests and watch
as the sleek, tiny adults clamber up a rocky cliff
and out into open view

binoculars land on noses
oohs and ahhs are extracted
a hush in twenty languages
is still a hush

the drama repeats, swim climb preen feed
hungry offspring become bolder as the darkness descends
crossing the fence and hassling the adults indiscriminately
creating comic relief
they don't really recognize their parents

by eleven everyone is yawning
a few photographers with tripods
slip in up front for the long haul
the rest of us gather our things
glance again at beach and sky
and begin to think about tomorrow's wonders

some events never really conclude

Wandering

Somewhere along the way
the cafes and museums become humdrum
I lose sight of my dreams
and hunger after a peaceful tomorrow
I begin to ache for a toothbrush in place by a sink
soap in the shower
a familiar bed

All the polyglot around me
once so very exciting
stops up my ears and makes it hard to breathe
"just go left, go right, and up the stairs...
you'll be fine," the locals chant
casting a knowing eye upward
at the approaching clouds

if you wander long enough
a clarity descends
if you don't
the world becomes a puddle of maps
edged in red, unpronounceable
each one pointing to a longing you must follow
or live with

I am approaching clear
I just have to go left, go right, go up the stairs
and remember to bring my raincoat

Eve

Everyday I pass by
tempted
the round perfect fruit
hanging low
nothing fallen
nothing to glean

"It's only an apple" I say to myself
but year after year
I check to see if her car is in the driveway
if there's a light on in the house

Chances are
I could cover the five feet from curb to tree
undetected
Chances are
I would be forgiven
Chances are
the world as we know it
would never be the same

Buttoned

If you are so different now
how come
I can draw you in
in the same way?

I am tired of being able to scare you
I would love to meet you
where I am
lifting, arching
taking more and more care
to move slowly into like and finally
love

it's a current of birds, crickets, grasshoppers
the flushness of summer
that once held us taut but now
I see you've backed away
buttoned your coat as if you could remove
all that I know about you

Landing

In this raging snowstorm
the first of winter
I move my body slowly
I experiment
here a joint that has stiffened
there a muscle or ligament
warning me with an ache

In the heat of summer
I fell
I tell my friends that I was making jungle love
but really I was changing
finding my way back to you
pushing through the crowds of twisted faces
anticipating the feel of that fleshy part of your hand
pushing solid against mine

perhaps I didn't fall so much as
land

The Only Borders I Ever Cross

For Nate Lowe

After you died
I took each of your love letters
dipped them into watery paste
and fashioned them into hands
white endless hands
that hold the words you wrote me
from the Sierras, from the Rockies
from the highest mountain tops in the world

Then I took water from icy streams
streams that you rode in kayaks and canoes
and I froze it into hands
white dripping hands
that slip into a waiting bucket
like the tears I worked up
from my memories, my bygones
the only places I ever go

the only borders I ever cross

Tracking

Amidst the junk mail and bills
just a thin white envelope
holding the weight of a life to come

Scribbled quickly in blue ball point pen
is the name of my daughter's kindergarten teacher
a kindly woman
on the verge of retirement

My breathing changes with visions and fears
is this the right place for her?
What about the vibrant young woman
with long dark hair?
a little plump
a big smile
wearing primary colors well

I try to imagine the first and second grade
Will they say that she is bright
talented
hard to handle?
Will she trade in her crayons for a lab coat
a ream of sheet music
a knight in shining armor
the future's equivalent of a flame and a spoon?

Who will take my girl to her prom?
a long dress of silk or taffeta
a moment too soon

They say it goes by in a snap
and surrounded by diapers and bottles
I did not believe them
until today
when I held the weight of her future
in a thin white envelope

Collect

Zawalo wakes us up a lot.
He calls at four A.M.
a startling moment
an operator speaking pidgin English
but no matter what time he calls
he always wants the same thing

Who can blame him for it?
In his mind, in his movies
we have so much
he doesn't know our gray skies
that everyone in America is trying to get rich too

he waits in line for a phone
has learned the word "collect"
and all of this connects him
to his only known hope

We don't exactly trust him
We're never sure where the money goes
but since the war that destroyed his country's postal system
we are helpless partners with the truth

Recently,
Zawalo found a FAX machine
he would have us push our dollar bills through the slot
and even a Xeroxed copy would be enough

Each time he wakes us up
I carry these thoughts through my day
I buy my coffee from a third world farm
and hope I am drinking hope...
not blood
or a great investment return

I wear my cotton T-shirts
drive my Japanese car
buy my produce at the co-op
answer my e-mail
and use my education

I stare into the abyss between our worlds
and trusting him is irrelevant
I long for the true solution
that would keep Zawalo
from waking us up a lot

Some Kind of Enough

I used to find a place to sit
and stare into God's face
an ocean
a canyon
a forest glen
but now I have you

noisy playgrounds
plastic toys and colorful books
all serve as props
for the light that bounces off your beautiful smile

Oh, my mind is busy
reminding me of the million and one important things
left undone
it is the message I am employed to resist
stay in the moment
stay so in the moment
that you cannot see her face change
from infant to toddler to girl child
her legs get strong and begin to clamber
her words get clear and
her message give you vision

if you notice these things
you have been too busy
if you notice these things
you cannot see God's face

only ocean
canyon
forest glen

and while they were once some kind of enough
they now pale in comparison

Yoga Now

For more than a quarter century
I postured daily
finding myself every morning
inside the tiny spaces between ligament and bone

my breath
filled the room
occasionally an errant engine outside
or a disrupting phone call

now
I hear her morning song
and I abandon myself
there is too much pleasure in "bukka bukka" and "gug"
words still so new
they mean nothing
and everything

For more than a quarter century
I held a moral high ground
willing to judge others
too busy to clean their houses
stretch their bodies

now
my muscles ache
from picking up toys
and trying to keep her in the same room
as whatever she may need
at any given moment

it's a new kind of union

thank God I took that time
thank God I'm giving it away

about the author

Bernice Lewis has been a national touring artist for almost three decades. She is a Singer/Songwriter, a published poet, a producer and a recording artist with six albums to her credit. She has worked with Dar Williams, Bobby McFerrin, Rosanne Cash, Guy van Duser, Peter. Paul, and Mary, the Dixie Chicks, Christine Lavin, Patty Griffin, Patty Larkin...the list is endless. She currently teaches songwriting at Williams College (Williamstown, MA) and Colorado College (Colorado Springs, CO), as well as at schools and retreat centers. In 2009 she was awarded an artist in residence position by the National Park Service. Her writings and recordings will be archived in the Southwest Collection at Texas Tech University in Lubbock, TX. She's had a thirty-year daily yoga practice, loves good coffee, and her religion is the Grand Canyon.

Previously published works include:

Appalachian Trailway News
American Zionist Movement Songbook
Open Ear Journal
Shots Magazine
Dermanities
The Resource Exchange Quarterly
Berkshire Eagle
Raven Review/Phantom Ranch
North Adams Transcript
Bone & Flesh
Coos County Democrat